# I Wish I Never Had a Teacher Like You!

Author **Zenobia Cockrell**

Illustrator **Anastasia Khmelevska**

© 2025 ZENOBIA COCKRELL. ALL RIGHTS RESERVED

No part of this book may be reproduced, stored in a retrieval system, or transmitted in any form or by any means electronic, mechanical, photocopy, recording, or otherwise, without the prior written permission of the publisher, except in the case of brief quotations used in reviews or articles.

ISBN 979-8-9930788-2-3
First Edition, 2025
Published by Zspire LLC
Lexington, MS
Printed in the United States of America

# DEDICATION

To God

Thank You for blessing me with the creative ideas and inspiration to write this story. May every word reflect the light You've placed in me.

Special thanks to my father, the late **Mr. Robert E. Lewis**, and to my beloved grandmothers, **Homer Lee Miller** and **Isabella Lewis**, who always believed in me and spoke greatness into my life.

To my incredible mother, Ms. Florine Lewis, and my supportive siblings—thank you for your love, your strength, and your encouragement.

And to the amazing students of **William Dean Jr. Elementary School** You are my biggest cheerleaders and the heart behind this story. Never stop shining.

With love and gratitude,

**Zenobia Cockrell**

Joy filled the air—it was a brand-new school year!
I was bursting with excitement, ready to cheer.
I couldn't wait to meet my teacher and friends,
Hoping for fun that never ends.

**As I walked in with a big, bright smile,**
My teacher frowned and stared for a while.
Still, I took that frown and turned it around,
**With a smile so wide, it lit up the ground!**

It spread through the room, across every face
My classmates lit up the whole classroom space.
It was contagious, like sunshine on cue.
But still...
**I wish I never had a teacher like you.**

On the very first day, I felt let down.
My teacher was rude and wore a deep frown.
But I lifted my head, looked up to the sky
My mom always told me to **hold my head high.**

Should I feel sad?
Maybe I should.
But I get glad because my classmates are good.
*Their smiles remind me of words Mom has said,*
*Words that dance in my heart when I go to bed.*

**I wish I never had a teacher like you.**
She says my name in such a harsh tone...
And I wish she'd just leave me alone.

But I softly recall how my mom says it right:
"**Your name is Zamiya—bright as the light.
It means blooming flower—smart, brave, and free.**
It means joy, and that's exactly what you'll always be."

**I'm her precious pearl, her pride, her delight**
Her brave little girl, who **shines so bright.**
Why can't my teacher see me that way too?
Is she just mean, like a bumblebee who
Spreads her wings, then lets out her stings?

I wish I never had a teacher like you.

So, I imagine **the teacher I one day will be**
One who sees the best in kids like me.
I'll greet each student with high fives and cheer,
Making sure they feel welcome and safe here.

From their head to their toes, they'll feel they belong
In a classroom filled with laughter all year long.
A place where their **confidence grows and grows...**

**I wish I had a teacher like me!**
And one day I will be that teacher
**so every child shines bright.**

# ACTIVITIES SECTION

### Note for Parents & Teachers

These activities are designed to help children connect with Zamiya's story in fun and meaningful ways.

- **Coloring Page:** Children can color Zamiya's bright school day and bring the scene to life.
- **Reflection Prompt:** Encourages children to imagine the kind of teacher they would like to be.
- **Rhyming Fun:** Builds early literacy skills by matching rhyming words.
- **Feelings Chart:** Helps children explore emotions and build social-emotional awareness.

Feel free to use these pages at home, in class, or as part of group storytime to spark conversations about kindness, confidence, and creativity.

# If I Were a Teacher

Draw or write how you would make your students feel welcome and happy.

------------------------------------------------------------

------------------------------------------------------------

------------------------------------

## RHYMING FUN

Draw a line to match the rhyming words in Column A to their rhyming partner in Column B.

| A | B |
|---|---|
| Smile | Light |
| Bright | Near |
| Cheer | Mile |

# FEELINGS CHART

Pick how Zamiya might have felt at different parts of the story

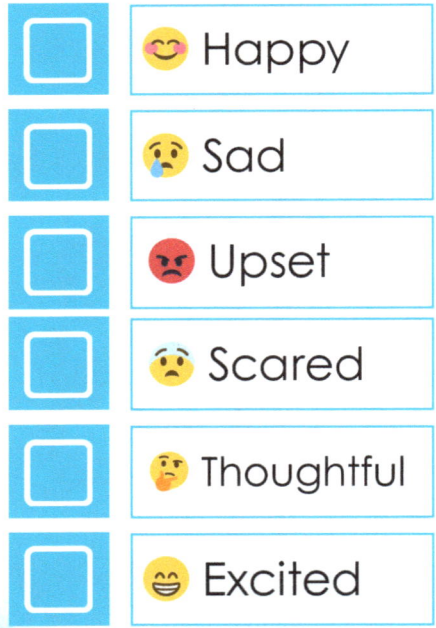

Keep shining, just like **Zamiya!**

www.ingramcontent.com/pod-product-compliance
Lightning Source LLC
Chambersburg PA
CBHW051515110526
44582CB00007B/126